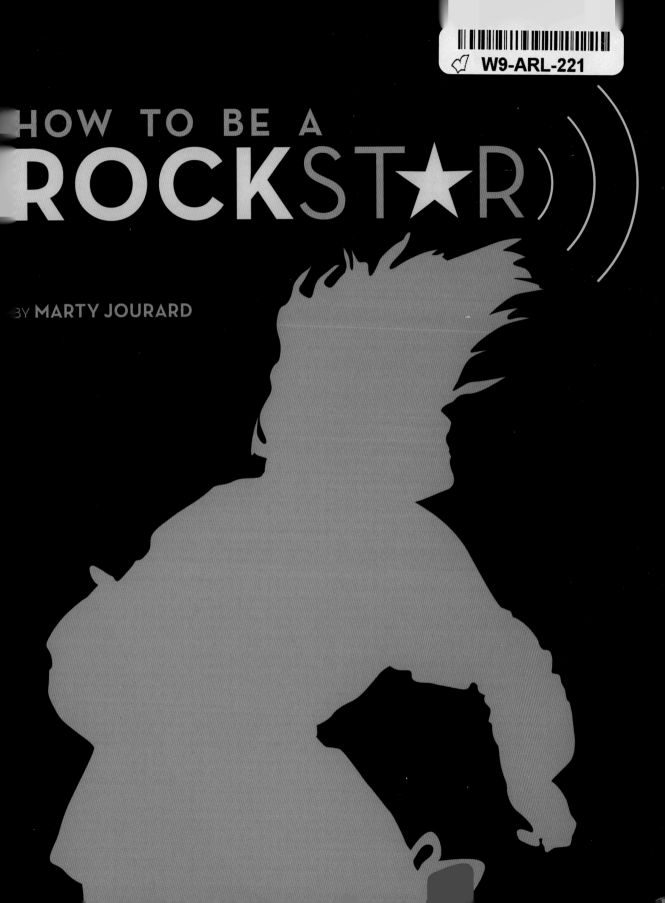

HOW TO BE A
ROCKST★R)

BY MARTY JOURARD

How to Be a Rock Star

by Marty Jourard

Produced by becker&mayer!, LLC
11010 Northup Way
Bellevue, WA 98004
www.beckermayer.com
If you have questions or comments about this product,
send e-mail to infobm@beckermayer.com.

How to Be a Rock Star is part of the *Rock Star Wireless Microphone Headset* kit.
Not to be sold separately.

an imprint of
SCHOLASTIC
www.scholastic.com

Scholastic and Tangerine Press and associated logos are trademarks of Scholastic Inc.

Published by Tangerine Press, an imprint of Scholastic Inc., 557 Broadway; New York, NY 10012

Edited by Nancy Waddell
Art direction and design by Scott Westgard
Illustrations by Ryan Hobson and Jim Steck
Assembly Illustrations by Ryan Hobson
Product development by Drew Barr and Mark Byrnes
Production management by Katie Stephens
Project management by Beth Lenz
Research assistance by Zena Chew

Image Credits: Page 6: *Green Day* Performing in Concert © John Atashian/CORBIS; Page 9: *U2* 's Singer Bono (R) and Group's Lead Guitarist, The Edge, Perform at Live 8 Concert © epa/Corbis; Page 15: GWEN STEFANI © Reuters/CORBIS; Page 16: Photos of the tracking room and control room at Ironwood Studios courtesy of Avast! Recording Co. Seattle.

M&M's is a registered trademark of Mars, Incorporated, a division of Masterfoods USA.

05396

ISBN: 0-439-87488-2

Printed, manufactured, and assembled in China.

10 9 8 7 6 5 4 3 2 1

IN TODAY'S WORLD, MUSIC IS EVERYWHERE—

ON THE RADIO AND TV, IN CARTOONS, MOVIES, VIDEOS, VIDEO GAMES, ON YOUR PERSONAL MUSIC PLAYER, AND AT LIVE PERFORMANCES. IF YOU LOVE MUSIC, YOU PROBABLY LISTEN TO YOUR FAVORITE SONGS EVERY DAY.

Listening to music is fun, but making music is even more fun. And what's the fastest and easiest way to start making music? By singing! Think about it—your voice is a musical instrument you already own. It didn't cost anything, and it's with you wherever you go. And, although musical trends come and go, singing is always in style.

Most singers began by singing along with their favorite songs. The Rock Star Microphone makes this easy and fun. Put it on, plug it in, and you'll hear your voice and the music coming through the speakers as if you are on the radio! And because the Rock Star Mic is hands-free, you can dance while you sing!

In the pages ahead we'll explore many subjects that will guide you in your musical journey. You'll learn the basics of songwriting, song structure, and how to take care of your voice. Then check out recording, touring, performing onstage, life on the road, and more.

TABLE OF CONTENTS

IF YOU LOVE TO SING AND ARE INTERESTED IN LEARNING MORE ABOUT MUSIC, **TURN THE PAGE.**

A song is a work of art made out of sound and words.

Songs are musical stories that are loaded with emotion. They can make you feel happy, sad, silly, excited, or almost any way at all. But songs don't just happen—someone has to write them. This someone could be you! The first step to writing songs is knowing how they are put together.

Let's look at the parts of a song.

Song Parts: VERSE CHORUS BRIDGE

Most songs have at least a **verse** and a **chorus**. Each verse in a song has the same melody but with different words. The chorus comes after the verse and has the same words and melody every time. A good chorus has a catchy melody that is easy to remember. If it is really catchy, you will go around all day singing it to yourself. The name of the song is often in the words of the chorus.

Here's a silly example. Remember singing "This Old Man" when you were little? The words in each verse are different, but the words in the chorus are always the same.

Verse 1:	This old man, he played one, He played knick-knack on my thumb
Chorus:	*With a knick-knack paddy whack, give a dog a bone, This old man came rolling home*
Verse 2:	This old man, he played two, He played knick-knack on my shoe
Chorus:	*With a knick-knack paddy whack, give a dog a bone, This old man came rolling home*
Verse 3:	This old man, he played three, He played knick-knack on my knee
Chorus:	*With a knick-knack paddy whack, give a dog a bone, This old man came rolling home*

The song "This Old Man" has the title in both the verse *and* the chorus. Songs usually put a chorus after every verse, over and over. But even a great verse and chorus will get old after a while. To make a song more interesting, sometimes a new musical part is added, called the bridge. This is a fresh piece of music that may have new words that add to the story. Not all songs have a bridge, but almost every song will have a verse and a chorus. Here is a typical song pattern:

Verse 1

Chorus

Verse 2

Chorus

BRIDGE

Verse 3

Chorus

TRYTHIS!

Songwriters think of songs as being "built" out of parts whose order can be changed. They spend a lot of time figuring it out. Listen to a favorite song and write down all the parts of the song from beginning to end. Then play around with the order. Does it change the meaning of the song when you move things around? Do you like your version better?

A good song has words and music that work together to convey an emotion.

One way to do this is to carefully choose the song's **tempo**—how fast or slow the music is played. A song about being excited or happy probably has a fast tempo; and a song about a peaceful or sad feeling often has a slow tempo.

How loud or soft you play parts of a song is called **dynamics**. You can mix it up within a song. For example, the verses can be quiet and gentle, and the chorus might be loud and crazy. Or, you can have a medium-tempo song gradually build in volume and intensity, such as "Boulevard of Broken Dreams" by *Green Day*.

Green Day Performing in Concert © John Atashian/CORBIS

A SONG CAN BE WRITTEN IN EITHER A MAJOR KEY OR A MINOR KEY.

Songs in major keys are built from a major scale, and songs in minor keys are built from a minor scale. Because of the nature of the sound, major keys are good for writing happier songs, while minor keys work better for songs about something serious, scary, or sad. But there are no "rules" about writing songs—you can write any song about anything in any key.

A to A
(Natural MINOR SCALE - *shown in yellow*)

SERIOUS, SCARY, or SAD

C to C
(MAJOR SCALE - *shown in purple*)

HAPPY

IDEAS for SONGS

An idea can be a song title ("Crazy Dream"), an important question ("Where's My Cat?"), things you like to do, like skateboarding ("Kickflip"), or a slang expression ("LOL," "Whatever…"). Sometimes you hear a song on the radio and get the words wrong. That's another great way to get new lyrics or a new idea!

Anything can inspire a song—a musical idea, a thought, a good or bad memory, or an emotion. Having a good imagination helps. *The Beatles* wrote a song called "Yellow Submarine" just because it was such a silly idea. Writing a song about how you feel not only feels good, but can also make someone else feel good when they hear it. Sometimes songs say things better than words.

HERE ARE SOME THINGS TO THINK ABOUT TO HELP YOU GET INSPIRED:

- Happy or sad things that have happened to you or a friend

- Things you wish would happen (a trip to an amusement park)

- Things you wish didn't happen (a trip to the principal's office)

- An adventure (camping, traveling)

- Places you have been (the mall, a toy store)

- Falling in love or out of love (this is a very popular subject!)

- Anything you can think of!

Collecting Your Song Ideas

Songwriters collect ideas for songs all the time and save them in a notebook or on a recorder. You can hum song melodies into a recorder and write the words later.

Become an observer. Notice how people walk and talk, what they wear, what they do, and how they react to things around them. Really good ideas often come to mind just before you go to sleep or just as you wake up, when your imagination is fresh. Make sure to always have a notepad and pencil close by. It is easy to forget your ideas. Write them down before they disappear.

SONGS ARE
MADE UP OF:
MUSIC (MELODY)
AND
WORDS (LYRICS).

Sometimes the melody comes first and sometimes the lyrics come first—it all depends on the song. If you have a musical idea and no words, think of a subject and then write down or sing the first thing that comes into your head. Don't worry about whether the words are good or bad. You can change them later. Keep trying until you come up with something you like. If you do this a lot, the words will flow.

If you have words but need the music, start singing your words, holding the sounds longer than if you were just reading them out loud. You can record your singing on a recorder (no one else has to hear it!), play it back, and keep the good stuff.

Sometimes you will come up with the words and music at the same time, for either a whole song or part of a song. Songs are written in all kinds of ways. Try them all. Remember—there is no "right" way to write a song.

COLLABORATING

When you write songs with someone and share your ideas, you are collaborating. Many famous songwriters work as a team—singer Bono of *U2* writes words to music by guitarist The Edge. If you and your partner can both write words and music, that is even better. John Lennon and Paul McCartney of *The Beatles* could both write words and music and would often help each other finish a song.

If you like to write music and your friend likes to write words (or the other way around), try writing songs together. At first it might feel funny because you are afraid your ideas aren't good enough. Don't worry—the other person might feel the same way! It's fun to write songs with other people. When it comes to songwriting, sometimes two heads are better than one.

U2's Singer Bono (r) and Group's Lead Guitarist, The Edge, Perform at Live 8 Concert © epa/Corbis

When you were a baby, you learned to talk by copying your parents. Learning how to sing or play music is the same. You listen and try to copy what you hear. This is the easiest way to learn music—most great rock performers started this way. The "copy songs you like" approach is really the best way to start out, because you are listening to music with "musician ears" instead of just for fun. But this can be more fun! In music school, they call this ear training—using your ears to figure out music.

The secret to learning by ear is selective listening—you only pay attention to the particular musical instrument you are

LEARNING THROUGH IMITATION

trying to learn. A singer only listens to the lead vocals. A drummer only listens to the drums, and a guitar player only listens to the guitar. They each ignore everything else in a song. Selective listening is a skill that really helps you play or sing your favorite songs.

Start with simple songs. When you get better at copying what you hear, you can try some harder songs. Rock 'n' roll songs from the 1950s are easy to figure out because they are very simple. Famous bands like *Green Day* and the *Rolling Stones* also have songs that are easy to learn. The more songs you learn from recordings, the easier it gets!

WHAT MUSIC LESSONS CAN AND CAN'T TEACH YOU

Music lessons are good for learning the basics, like scales, singing properly, and how to read **music notation** (notes and stuff). Because singing uses your vocal cords, a good teacher will show you how to sing—or better yet, scream!—without hurting your throat.

Music lessons can teach you things that would take a long time to figure out by yourself. Many famous performers, like Alicia Keys, Elton John, and Tori Amos, started out with classical piano lessons. Although rock and pop music are different from classical music, all music uses scales, chords, and rhythms. So a lot of what you learn in music class can help you play and sing your favorite songs. Finding a good teacher is important. But in any case, make sure you learn a lot of songs. Practice the words until you have them memorized. There is no substitute for practicing! The total of all the songs you can perform is called your **repertoire** (rep-er-TWAR).

Music lessons can only take you so far. Then you take what you learned and start to develop your own musical style. Finding your own style will happen naturally as you play more and more. Your style will evolve as you continue your musical journey.

MUSIC—

Music is made up of

YOU DON'T HAVE TO READ MUSIC TO PLAY MUSIC, BUT IT MAKES IT EASIER TO LEARN SONGS.

There are many books and software programs that can teach you how to read music, but here are the basics.

Music is made up of two parts: sound and silence. Music is written out on five lines (called the staff) using notes to indicate sound and rests to indicate silence.

SOME NOTES ON NOTES

- Every note has a certain pitch—low notes, high notes—and the pitch of a note depends on where you put it on the musical staff.

- A note will either be on a line or in a space.

- Notes on the bottom of the staff are lower in pitch than notes on the top of the staff.

HIGH NOTES

LOW NOTES

NOTES

The length of time you play a note is shown by what the note looks like.

There are other kinds of notes, but these are the most common:

WHOLE NOTE
Play the note for four beats.

HALF NOTE
Play the note for two beats.

QUARTER NOTE
Play the note for one beat.

EIGHTH NOTE
Play the note for a half beat.

READING BASICS

two basic parts: SOUND and SILENCE
NOTES and RESTS

RESTS

Rests are musical symbols that show the length of silence.

WHOLE REST

Rest for four beats.

HALF REST

Rest for two beats.

QUARTER REST

Rest for one beat.

EIGHTH REST

Rest for half a beat.

Guitar Tab

There is a special kind of notation called guitar tab (short for tablature) or just tab. The six lines represent guitar strings, and the numbers tell you what guitar fret to press on each string to make guitar chords or melodies ("leads" or "solos").

This tab tells you to put your fingers on the second fret, the third fret, and the second fret of the top three strings on the guitar. This makes a D major chord. You can find books and websites with entire songs in tab. Many singers learn a few basic guitar chords to help them write and sing songs.

1st fret
2nd fret
3rd fret
4th fret

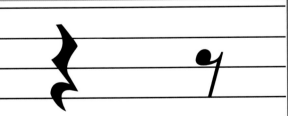

Guitar Tablature

SINGING

Singing is mostly holding out vowel sounds (a, e, i, o, u). If you don't believe me, first sing the vowel "eeeee," and then try to sing the letter "k"! Practice singing vowel sounds in various pitches.

Every singer has a natural vocal range—the lowest and highest note they can sing. To reach all these notes, you use your normal voice and your falsetto, which feels different and allows you to sing even higher. Everyone has a certain note where they switch to falsetto. Great singers can switch without anyone noticing, but you have to work on your falsetto so it sounds full and natural.

SINGING IS MOSTLY HOLDING OUT VOWEL SOUNDS (A, E, I, O, U).

You need to warm up your voice before you sing because you can hurt your vocal cords from singing too loud, too hard, or too long. Many singers drink herbal tea with lemon and honey to warm their throat before they sing. Singing involves not only your vocal cords, but also your overall posture, your lungs, and the muscles around your stomach. It is even affected by where you place your feet. If you want to be a singer, you should sing whenever you can. Join a school chorus or a choir where you can get lots of practice.

HOW DO YOU KNOW IF YOU ARE ANY GOOD?
DOES IT MATTER?

Who decides if you are "good" at singing or playing? Whose opinion do you trust? Your parents? Your friends? Your brother or sister? When you are starting out, does it even matter what other people think? Probably not. The reason is this: You will always be more skilled than one person and less skilled than another. So everyone is in the middle somewhere! Performing music is not a contest—it is a lifelong adventure. Keep singing, and don't spend any time worrying about whether you are "good" or not.

GWEN STEFANI © Reuters/CORBIS

IN THE **STUDIO**

A PROFESSIONAL RECORDING STUDIO HAS SEVERAL ROOMS.

The band sets up and plays in the tracking room. The recording equipment is in a separate control room. Both rooms have soundproofed walls, so the recording engineer only hears what comes through the microphones into the mixing board, and then the studio monitors (speakers). Making a good recording in a studio takes time and skill because a microphone doesn't hear things the way our ears do. It hears them even better! The littlest mistake shows up when the song is played back. Bands and singers rehearse their songs a lot before they go into the studio.

TRACKING ROOM

CONTROL ROOM

MULTITRACK RECORDING

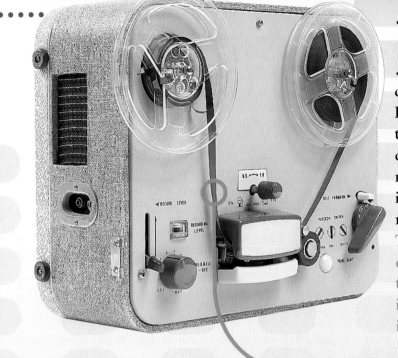

In the early days of recording, everyone in the band played all at once into one or maybe two microphones. If one player made a mistake, the recording had to be done over again. Then in the 1950s, multitrack recording was invented. Each instrument is recorded on a separate "track." Think of a striped ribbon with each stripe being a different track for a separate musical instrument, and you'll get the idea.

If a musician makes a mistake, that track can be changed later without changing the other tracks. If the band played perfectly but the vocal track was out of tune, the vocal track can be re-recorded later. The singer wears headphones to hear the music from the recording and sings along as if it were live. The microphone only picks up the singing, not what is in the headphones. When the engineer records the new vocal on the track, it automatically erases the old vocal. Cool, huh?

Redoing a part or adding a new part on a recording is called overdubbing, and a song may have 48 or more separate tracks that can be erased or changed. When the song parts are finished, the song is mixed to adjust the volume of each track so it sounds perfect.

TRACK 1: LEAD VOCALS
TRACK 2: BACKUP VOCALS
TRACK 3: GUITAR 1
TRACK 4: GUITAR 2
TRACK 5: BASS
TRACK 6: DRUMS

THE STEPS LIVE BAND

STEP 1:

The instruments and recording gear are set up in the tracking room—drums, guitars, amplifiers, keyboards, microphones, and cables.

STEP 2:

The guitars and drums are tuned.

STEP 3:

Microphones are adjusted for volume and position.

STEP 7:

The band records the song over and over until they are happy with their performance.

STEP 8:

If anyone makes a mistake, they fix it by either a "punch-in" (fixing a single mistake) or by re-doing the entire part.

STEP 9:

Overdubs (new parts) are added, such as background vocals ("oooohhhh") or guitar solos, or any cool musical ideas.

STEP 4:

Everybody puts on headphones so they can hear everyone else.

STEP 5:

The recording engineer starts the recorder, the drummer counts to four, and the band begins to play.

STEP 6:

The singer sings a guide vocal so everyone knows where he or she is in the song. This vocal track can be re-recorded later.

STEP 10:

Listening to the recording, the singer sings along with the finished track and gets a perfect vocal recording.

STEP 11:

The completed song is mixed so the sound is balanced.

STEP 12:

Repeat steps 1-11 until you have enough songs to fill a CD.

CONGRATULATIONS!
YOU JUST MADE
AN ALBUM!

THE BEST WAY A BAND CAN IMPROVE THEIR PERFORMING SKILLS AND ATTRACT NEW FANS IS TO PLAY ONSTAGE IN DIFFERENT CITIES. THE VARIETY OF VENUES INCLUDES CLUBS, THEATERS, MUSIC FESTIVALS, CONCERT HALLS, COLLEGE AUDITORIUMS, COUNTY FAIRS, AND—WHEN YOU GET REALLY BIG—SPORTS ARENAS AND STADIUMS.

PUTTING A SHOW ON THE ROAD TAKES **MORE THAN JUST THE SINGER AND THE BAND.** HERE ARE SOME OF THE PEOPLE WHO MAKE IT HAPPEN.

ROAD MANAGER

TODAY IS: Wednesday, July 14   TRAVEL AND SHOW DAY

TRAVEL INFORMATION
BUS WILL DEPART PAWTUCKET, RI AFTER SHOW
APPROX. 2:00 AM
DRIVE 95 MILES. ARRIVE HARTFORD, CT 4:00AM

HOTEL INFORMATION
GOVERNOR'S HOUSE HOTEL
440 WALNUT
HARTFORD, CT 06103
203/555-6591

VENUE: 15 MILES
AIRPORT: 20 MINS. (BRADLEY)
ROOM SERVICE: NONE
HOLDING 11 SINGLES

COFFEE SHOP/RESTAURANT: 3:00 PM - 10:00 PM
24 HR RESTAURANT: RYAN'S DELI LOCATED IN CIVIC CENTER

SHOW INFORMATION
VENUE: AGORA BALL ROOM
         HARTFORD, CT

PROMOTER: BOBBY WALDEN 216/555-1231

LOAD IN: 1:00 PM
SOUND CHECK: 4:30 PM
SHOW TIME: 9:00 PM
CAPACITY: 1,200 people

Road manager's sample itinerary

The **ROAD MANAGER**'s job is to make sure that everyone on the tour is doing his or her job. Even though they work for the performers, the road manager is the "boss" of the tour. They keep the musical act informed of the day's events—what time they need to wake up, if there is an interview or in-store appearance to promote the show, when to get onstage, how long to play, where to go after the show (the bus? the airport? back to the hotel?), and where to get a pizza at three in the morning. Everybody on the tour is given a tour itinerary that explains where they are, what they are supposed to do, and when they need to do it. A few weeks on the road can turn everything into a blur, and the itinerary tells them important stuff like what day it is and the name of the city they're in!

The **SOUND TECHNICIAN** is in charge of the mixing board and the stacks of speaker cabinets on either side of the stage. Before each show, the sound tech has the band do a sound check, where the volume and tone of each instrument is carefully adjusted. Each musician waits his or her turn and when asked, plays or sings. Then everyone plays together and the overall mix is adjusted. The level of the monitors is also adjusted. The monitors are speakers on the floor or the side of the stage aimed at the performers so they can hear each other. Some performers use tiny ear monitors that are custom-fitted to the shape of their ears. Sound check is very important, and some acts will spend two hours to get everything sounding right.

The **STAGE MANAGER** makes sure all the onstage sound equipment and musical gear is properly set up, including the lighting and special effects like fog machines. He or she will put glow-in-the-dark tape on the steps leading up to the stage so the performers know where to walk, and hand everyone a towel and a bottle of water when they head for the dressing room after the show. The stage manager watches the whole show from the side of the stage to make sure everything is running smoothly.

ROAD CREW aka "Roadies"

ROADIES DO MOST OF THE PHYSICAL WORK LIKE HEAVY LIFTING.

The **ROAD CREW** are the people who do most of the physical work like heavy lifting. They unload all the sound and light gear from the truck, set it up properly, make sure the guitars are tuned and the band gear is in the right place, then pack everything up after the show and drive the truck to the next city to do it all over again.

WHY SO MANY GUITARS?

WHAT'S WITH ALL THOSE GUITARS? EACH GUITAR HAS A DIFFERENT SOUND, AND A PARTICULAR SONG MAY NEED AN ACOUSTIC GUITAR OR AN ELECTRIC GUITAR. SPARE GUITARS ARE NEARBY IN CASE THE GUITARIST BREAKS A STRING IN THE MIDDLE OF A SONG. AND SOME GUITARS JUST LOOK SO COOL, THE GUITARIST HAS TO PLAY IT IN FRONT OF THE AUDIENCE!

BACKSTAGE—WHO AND WHAT IS THERE?

BACKSTAGE
IS WHERE YOU GO TO HANG OUT BEFORE AND AFTER THE SHOW. ONLY INVITED FRIENDS AND VISITORS WEARING A BACKSTAGE PASS CAN GET PAST THE SECURITY GUARDS.

BACKSTAGE PASS

ViP

TOUR RIDERS

EVERY MUSICAL ACT HAS A TOUR RIDER—A LIST OF EXTRA THINGS A BAND OR PERFORMER WANTS THE CONCERT PROMOTER TO PROVIDE FOR THEIR PERFORMANCE. SOME BANDS ASK FOR THE CRAZIEST THINGS! HERE ARE SOME EXAMPLES.

ARTIST	BACKSTAGE REQUEST
Van Halen	Bowl of M&M's with all the brown ones removed (really!)
Moby	10 pairs of socks, 10 pairs of underwear
Christina Aguilera	Bottle of Flintstones multivitamins with extra C
50 Cent	Two dozen shrimp on ice, two dozen pieces KFC chicken
'N Sync	Pop-Tarts, Cap'n Crunch cereal, Oreo O's cereal
New Kids on the Block	4 quarts Häagen-Dazs ice cream
Elton John	Large arrangement of flowers (no chrysanthemums, lilies, carnations, or daisies!)
Snoop Dogg	Sony PlayStation, vanilla ice cream ("very important")

WHO SELLS THE T-SHIRTS?

ROCK 'N' ROLL! WORLD TOUR 2006

Who pays $25 for a T-shirt? Fans! The money you spend on an "official" T-shirt is split among the musical act, the company that makes the shirts, and the venue. There is a lot of money in T-shirts and other official merchandise, and some tours have people whose only job is to keep track of all the stuff and sell it. Often there are cheap "bootleg" shirts on sale outside of the concert, but they are poorly made as well as illegal—only the performers have the right to sell their likeness or logo on shirts and other merchandise.

SMOKE AND MIRRORED LEMONS

◆◆◆◆◆◆◆◆◆◆◆◆◆

A concert isn't just about the music. Performers often make wild entrances or do crazy stunts to keep the crowd excited. On one tour by superstars *U2*, a 40-foot mirror-ball lemon rolled into the crowd, the top cracked open, and the band popped out chanting "Boom-Cha!" Country superstar Garth Brooks appeared to fly at one point in his show thanks to hidden wires and a body harness—and steady nerves! Jimi Hendrix lit his guitar on fire at a rock festival (don't try this at home!) and *The Who* were famous for destroying all of their instruments after each show.

Light shows can be crazy, too, thanks to lasers, fog and smoke machines, computer-driven lights that move to the music, and giant TV screens above the stage. Fireworks and other special effects that involve fire and heat are called pyrotechnics and require a special crew to keep everyone onstage—and in the audience—safe from harm.

SINGING + DANCING = CHOREOGRAPHY

Before music videos, a musician would play an instrument, or sing, or do both. With a regular microphone on a stand, they had to stay in one place or carry it around. Then along came MTV. Now, **MANY SINGERS PERFORM COMPLICATED DANCE MOVES AS THEY SING.** How do they do that? By hiring a choreographer—a professional dancer who comes up with cool dance routines and teaches the singer and other dancers what to do. You need to be in excellent physical shape to dance and sing at the same time. And you need a hands-free microphone.

With a wireless microphone—just like your ROCK STAR MICROPHONE—you can dance while you sing.

LEAD A SING-ALONG

A cool trick when performing is to have the audience sing the chorus of your song along with you. Just raise both your hands up and shout out, "Everybody!" before each chorus and then put one hand behind an ear like you are listening to them. Then scream, "I can't hear you!" and watch what happens.

OPENING ACT

Being the opening act on a big tour is a great opportunity. The headliner is doing you a favor by letting you play to a bigger audience—their audience! They know it and you know it, so don't try to be pushy. And don't be surprised if you don't get a sound check, if they don't let you use their light show, if they only give you 27 minutes to play, and if you get a very small dressing room. If you are nice, they might invite you to the end-of-the-tour party. Be nice. There are plenty of other artists who want to be opening for a big act.

SURF THE CROWD

Surfing the crowd means jumping into the front row of a standing audience that has crowded to the front of the stage. With luck, they will hold you up with their arms after you jump and pass you over their heads from one person to the next. You might get dropped, though, so crowd-surf at your own risk!

HECKLERS

are people in the audience who want attention. But since they aren't onstage, they yell and try to interrupt the show. The best thing to do is ignore them. If that doesn't work, you can always try a few classic comebacks:

"Hey, I don't come to your job and help you flip burgers."

"We already played that one." (Say this over and over again no matter what they yell. They'll think you're crazy.)

"Hey, one of us is onstage with a mic! Is it me...or you?"

"It's way past your bedtime. Better go home..."

If you keep playing songs, there won't be any time for hecklers to say anything, so keep the show going.

FAME AND FANS

is music a contest?

is FAME success?

everybody wants to be well-known and admired.

If enough people feel this way about you, you become famous. But fame is different from talent, and some people have a hard time separating the two.

Every musician has his or her own style of singing or playing. Some people can sing in high tones, some people sing in low tones. Some people have a pure sound, and some sing rough and bluesy. TV shows like *American Idol* can make music seem like a race or a contest with only one way to sing that will make you a winner who becomes famous. Winning any contest is always a big thrill, but music is much, much bigger than any television show or contest! Anyone who spends time learning music, playing music, and enjoying music is a winner.

Fame is not something you can control. A singer can be doing the same thing he or she always does and suddenly become famous for it. Then fame moves on to the next person. What you can control is your talent and how hard you work at becoming a good musician or singer. Fame can come and go, but your love of music and your ability to sing and play can't be taken away from you.

Another funny thing about fame: If you aren't famous, you really want to be, but famous people sometimes wish they weren't. Fame has its problems, too. Why? Because famous people like to do normal things just like you do, and fame makes that difficult. Many famous people would like go to the store or walk down the street without being noticed, having their photo taken, or being asked for an autograph. It might be hard to understand when you are starting out, but fame can also be a hassle!

★ Being interviewed ★

What is it like to be interviewed, to have someone ask all about you and your life and your music? It can be fun! There are many types of interviews. The music writer for a newspaper or magazine can meet you before a concert or at a recording session and ask questions. You could go to a television studio or radio station and have your interview recorded for broadcast later, or go on the air "live." There are also interviews called "phoners" where you don't meet the person interviewing you but just talk on the phone. Famous people get used to interviews, but sometimes they get asked really silly questions.

GET READY FOR YOUR INTERVIEW!

You are a singer with a new record, a hot new video, and a soon-to-be world tour. A reporter asks you these questions. What would you say?

★ What do your songs mean?

★ What's it like being famous?

★ Are you dating the singer from *Crazylips*?

★ What do you do in the morning?

★ Do you like to sing?

★ What is your favorite junk food?

★ How can we achieve world peace?

★ If you were a tree, what kind of tree would you be?

a Final word

If you really love to sing and play, music can open the door to a whole new world. You will meet new people, travel to new places, and become part of the

follow your dreams

global family of musicians and performers. Have fun with it. If you work on your skills and follow your dream, good things will always come your way.

ASSEMBLY INSTRUCTIONS

Your **ROCK STAR MICROPHONE** is like a mini FM radio station and sound mixer all in one. How is this possible? The transmitter combines your voice from the microphone and your music, from your MP3 or CD player, into one signal, and then transmits it to your radio.

The mixer is controlled by the white dial marked "MUSIC/VOICE," which allows you to blend your voice with your music. Just like a sound engineer at a concert or in the studio, you can adjust the levels to get the best possible sound. As you build and test your Rock Star Mic, you'll have a chance to test the clarity of your voice, balance your music, and experiment with mixing them together.

YOUR KIT INCLUDES:

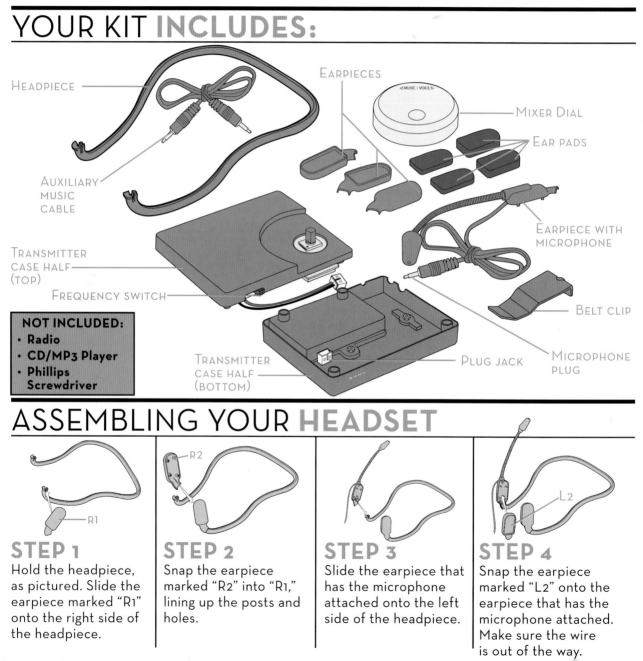

- Headpiece
- Earpieces
- Mixer Dial
- Ear pads
- Auxiliary Music Cable
- Transmitter Case Half (Top)
- Frequency switch
- Earpiece with Microphone
- Belt clip
- Transmitter Case Half (Bottom)
- Plug jack
- Microphone Plug

NOT INCLUDED:
- Radio
- CD/MP3 Player
- Phillips Screwdriver

ASSEMBLING YOUR HEADSET

STEP 1
Hold the headpiece, as pictured. Slide the earpiece marked "R1" onto the right side of the headpiece.

STEP 2
Snap the earpiece marked "R2" into "R1," lining up the posts and holes.

STEP 3
Slide the earpiece that has the microphone attached onto the left side of the headpiece.

STEP 4
Snap the earpiece marked "L2" onto the earpiece that has the microphone attached. Make sure the wire is out of the way.

STEP 5

There are two sets of ear pads to choose from. One set is thicker than the other. Before you remove the tape, test out each set to see which best fits your head.

Put the pads on the insides of the earpieces, hold them down in place, and put the headset on, as pictured.

STEP 6

Once you've decided which set of ear pads to use, remove the tape on both of them and stick them onto the insides of the earpieces.

ASSEMBLING YOUR TRANSMITTER

STEP 1

With the case halves open and facing upward, as pictured, plug the wire into the plug jack. Make sure the groove is facing outward. It only fits one way.

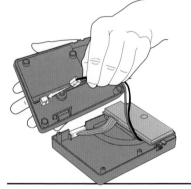

STEP 2

Snap case halves together, lining up the posts and holes.

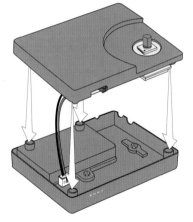

STEP 3

The flat edge on the bottom of the mixer dial lines up with the flat edge of the post on the transmitter. Snap the mixer dial into the transmitter, as shown.

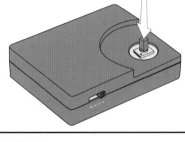

STEP 4

Unscrew the battery door and insert three 1.5 volt AAA batteries into the back of the transmitter. Be sure to position them correctly, as shown.

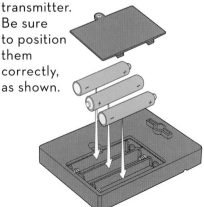

STEP 5

Screw on the battery door. Switch on the transmitter to make sure you've built it correctly so far. It's working if the light comes on!

STEP 6

Place the belt clip into its designated slot. Screw it on.

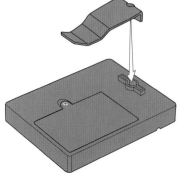

The belt clip will need to be removed every time you replace the batteries.

TUNING YOUR TRANSMITTER

The Rock Star Microphone works on almost all radios—on your boom box, on your stereo radio receiver, and even in the car. Remember, you are not going to sing along to music from your local radio station. You are creating your own radio station!

When you tune your radio, using the following steps, you are searching for the FM signal that your transmitter is sending out. If another radio station in your area is sending a signal out at the same frequency, you will not be able to receive a clear signal from your transmitter. That is why your transmitter has four different channels that it can send signals on.

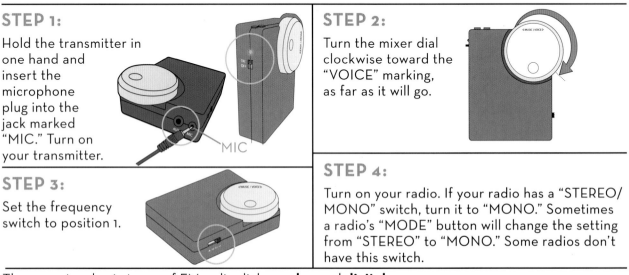

STEP 1:

Hold the transmitter in one hand and insert the microphone plug into the jack marked "MIC." Turn on your transmitter.

STEP 2:

Turn the mixer dial clockwise toward the "VOICE" marking, as far as it will go.

STEP 3:

Set the frequency switch to position 1.

STEP 4:

Turn on your radio. If your radio has a "STEREO/MONO" switch, turn it to "MONO." Sometimes a radio's "MODE" button will change the setting from "STEREO" to "MONO." Some radios don't have this switch.

There are two basic types of FM radio dials: **analog** and **digital**.

If your radio looks like this, it's an analog radio:

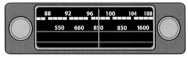

If your radio looks like this, it's a digital radio:

STEP 5: ANALOG INSTRUCTIONS

If your radio has an analog dial, slowly turn the knob from 97.0 FM to 98.0 FM until you find a clear zone of silence. Speak or blow into the microphone, or tap it a few times with your finger. If you hear this sound coming through your radio speakers, your Rock Star Mic is tuned to your radio! MAKE SURE YOU TURN THE DIAL VERY SLOWLY, OR YOU COULD MISS THE SETTING TO MATCH UP WITH YOUR ROCK STAR MIC!

STEP 5: DIGITAL INSTRUCTIONS

If your radio has a digital display, tune it to 97.0 FM. Tap the "TUNER UP" button up to 98.0 FM, or until you find a clear zone of silence. Speak or blow into the microphone, or tap it a few times with your finger. If you hear this sound coming through your radio speakers, your Rock Star Mic is tuned to your radio! TAP THE "TUNER UP" BUTTON SO THE FREQUENCY JUMPS UP ONE NUMBER AT A TIME. FOR EXAMPLE, 97.0 TO 97.1, 97.1 TO 97.2, ETC. OR YOU COULD MISS THE SETTING TO MATCH UP WITH YOUR ROCK STAR MIC!

Did you find a clear channel? If yes—go to step 7. If no—go to step 6.

STILL NEED HELP FINDING A CHANNEL? TRY THIS!

If you don't find a clear zone of silence or hear your voice, place the microphone right next to the speaker, and increase the volume of your radio. Finely tune your radio, listening for feedback (a loud squeal or hum). If you move the microphone a few feet away from the speaker, the feedback should go away. If the feedback goes away, speak into the microphone—you should hear your voice. Move the radio dial up and down a tiny bit to make sure you have the clearest channel selected. If you're happy with this channel, skip to Step 7.

If you don't find a clear zone of silence, hear your voice, or find any feedback by the time you get to 98.2, then you'll need to try another setting on your microphone (go to step 6).

STEP 6:

Turn the frequency switch to position 2. Set the tuner on your radio to 97.8 FM and try step 5 again. If you get to 99.0 FM and can't find a clear zone of silence, hear your voice, or find any feedback, then try setting the frequency switch on your transmitter to position 3, and tune your radio to frequencies between 98.6 FM to 99.8 FM. Position 4 on the frequency switch has frequencies from 99.4 FM to 100.6 FM. You should be able to find a setting on your radio using one of these four frequency ranges.

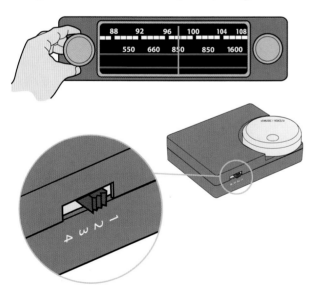

STEP 7:

Place the assembled headset over your head and around your ears so that the soft foam padding rests against the sides of your head comfortably.

Line up the microphone so that it is directly in front of your mouth.

Make sure to speak right into the holes of the microphone.

STEP 8:

Test your microphone. Stand four to six feet from your radio and speak into your microphone: "Test one, test two." If you have a good signal, you should hear your voice clearly coming from the radio.

FREQUENCY RANGES

Position #1:	97.0 FM – 98.0 FM
Position #2:	97.8 FM – 99.0 FM
Position #3:	98.6 FM – 99.8 FM
Position #4:	99.4 FM – 100.6 FM

Go to www.beckermayer.com/support.html for further tips and hints.

PLUGGING IN YOUR MP3 OR CD PLAYER

STEP 1:

Keep your radio tuned to the same station as before.

Included with your Rock Star Mic is an auxiliary music cable. Take either end of the cable and plug it into the jack on your transmitter labeled "AUX."

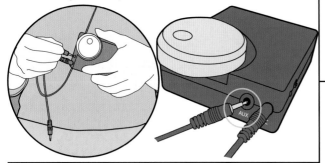

STEP 2:

Use the belt clip to attach the transmitter to your belt or waistband.

STEP 3:

Take the other end of the auxiliary music cable and plug it into the headphone jack of your MP3 or CD player.

Turn on your MP3 or CD player and set the volume to about 3/4.

STEP 4:

Turn the mixer dial counterclockwise toward the "MUSIC" marking, as far as it will go. To test this, turn on your MP3 or CD player and play your favorite song. You should hear only your music from your MP3 or CD player coming through your radio.

STEP 5:

Every personal music player is going to act differently with the Rock Star Mic. Test yours by experimenting with the volume on your MP3 orCD player. There will be less chance of sound distortion at a particular volume.

STEP 6:

Turn the mixer dial clockwise halfway back from the "MUSIC" only position, and sing into your microphone. The volume of your voice should be about the same as the volume of your music.

MINI EXPERIMENT: MIXING

Experiment with mixing music and voice levels. Alternately turn the mixer dial toward "MUSIC" and toward "VOICE" until you find your preferred mix.

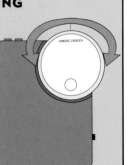

Now that you have built, tuned, and tested your Rock Star Microphone, you're ready to rock!